HEY, THERE'S A ZOO ON MY FRONT PORCH!

Shelia L. Anderson

Drawings and Graphic Editing by J. David Frasier

HEY, THERE'S A ZOO ON MY FRONT PORCH!

"Hello, my sad-faced neighbor and friend!
What, my dear, is the matter with you?"

"My mommy said she can't take me to the zoo!
Says she just has too much to do.
And my dad says he has to work, too."

1

"Oh, your zoo must be in a far-away town,
or maybe there just aren't any zoos to be found.
But maybe if you open wide your eyes,
you all may have a big surprise!"

"I have some good news for you!
How would you like to come to my

Front Porch Zoo?

When you see what's in store,

you won't be sad anymore.

Come, walk with me next door.

Let's visit the zoo on my **Front porch!**"

3

"I don't believe you.
Really? A zoo? On the porch?
You've stayed in the sun too long.
Your brain must be scorched!"

"Aren't you a teeny, tiny bit curious to see
if this zoo can actually be?
Bring your imagination and come along with me."

"My Front Porch Zoo has no cages or bars,
so, I must attract my guests with lots of
beautiful flowers."

"No cages or bars? Isn't that dangerous?"
"Not at all. The animals are free to do as they please.
But with a zoo like this, why would they leave?"

5

"See the pretty, peachy orchid?
With its bright, thick, green leaves,
it's sure to please
hungry little bugs and
caterpillars, too.
They scallop the leaves' edges
and eat holes clean through!"

caterpillar

"These insects I can see with my eyes.
Some, though, come with great disguises!
I almost passed this caterpillar and stick bug
right by!"

"So, now what do you have to say?"

"It's nice to have these Flowers galore.
It's too bad these bugs are herbivores!"

"Yes, you are absolutely right!
But let's take a look at some other
Fascinating sights!"

7

"Did you know that some bugs eat bugs?
Yes, indeed, they are not all smiles and hugs!
Of course, I need them to keep things just right
in my Front Porch Zoo.
Without my bug-eaters,
I don't know what I would do!"

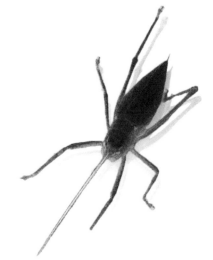

"With his front legs folded, this
praying mantis appears to be
praying for prey!
At least it sure looks that way."

"These assassin bugs look fierce!
They use their long thin beak to
pierce!
Aren't you glad you're not a bug?
Oh, my! Ugh!"

8

"And speaking of bug-eating bugs..."

daddy long legs

wolf spider

"Wow! Look at that big brown spider!
My mom would never let that get near her!"

"It's big all right!
Its size surprised me, too!
It had to be a part of my Front Porch Zoo!"

Banana spider traps
lunch...a grasshopper!

"Spiders have a Fancy name, too:
Arachnid–a-rach-nid.

They are bugs with eight legs,
because unlike other bugs,
six legs For them just wouldn't do! "

"Most spiders are harmless,
but you never Know.
So if you're not sure, just let it go."

"Next up is our serpentarium
Come on, don't stand there mum!
You can say it: ser-pen-ta-ri-um.
There, can you see it?
A beautiful little snake!
There, in my Flower pot,
with brown, yellow, and white spots
just keeping cool, and not too hot!

Now, snakes are sort of like
spiders.
If you're not sure of its kind,
Just leave it behind!"

"Wow, who knew?
This is beginning to look like a zoo!"

"Now, is this not the cutest thing
you've ever seen?
A pretty little Frog,
all dressed in green!"

"He is so nice,
let's look at him twice!"
But he's not just cute,
he has work to do.
He's a great little bug-eater, too!

12

"Oh, yes! There is another thing that's green:
Its Fancy name is the green anole, "ah-no-lee,"
but we all mostly call it a lizard."

"I hope this doesn't sound too mean. But why
does your zoo have so much green?"
"Well, this is after all, a Front porch zoo.
I don't have the exact answer today.
Let's just say God made it that way.
But if you would just stick around,
you can see something green turn to brown!"

Peek-a-boo, I see you.

Do you see me, too?

Stunning green necklace you're wearing!

14

"Hey, does you zoo have anything that Flies?"

"Does it ever! It will be a Feast For your eyes!"

"Ugh! What's that Furry thing?!"

"That's exactly what I said, too,

when he First showed up at my porch zoo!

It's too small to be a bear;

with no wings, it can't be a bat.

Touch it? I wouldn't dare!

That Furry thing gave me quite a scare!

So I had to study and dig around,

and you wouldn't believe what I Found!

This Furry critter is a **puss moth caterpillar**!

Speaking of moths..."

Puss moth caterpillar

"Ta-duh! Look at this beauty! Amazing, huh?"

"Absolutely amazing!"

pink striped oak moth

clymeme haploa moth

"A moth is sort of like a butterfly,
with some differences,
but don't ask me why!"

"Maybe it's so nighttime animals
won't feel left out
of the beauty of daytime butterflies
that always flutter about."
"Hey, good idea! I never thought of that!"

fan-tailed moth

17

"By golly, I think you're right!
Moths must be butterflies
Equipped for the night!"

"But just between you and me, my friend,
butterflies or moths, I like them both the same!"

19

A zoo would not be complete without birds!
A place for birds is called an *aviary, a-vee-er-ree,*
And they are not at all scary!
But they can be very busy!

"My Front Porch Zoo has a Family of wrens.

They spy my beautiful flower baskets, and move right in.

And my stuff that they don't need,

out they throw it!

Mulch, soil, flowers, and moss,

if wrens don't want them,

they are all tossed!

And for me, I feel some pain

because my gardening money

goes down the drain!"

"But before you know it,
what an amazing sight!
A cute little hollowed-out home
in the warm sunlight!"

"Now all is ready for moving in day,

and one by one, Mom Wren her eggs begin to lay;

Five or six brown spotted little pearls.

Who knows? Maybe three boys and three girls!"

23

"It won't take long and before you know,
little Furry hatchlings begin to show!

With mouths wide open and eyes aglow,
they watch and wait for Mom and Pop,
who all day long come and go!
With lots of food to help their chicks grow!"

"And grow they do!

One by one, plop, plop, plop—

out of the nest they begin to drop!

They Flit and Flitter and Flap their little wings,

and it doesn't take long until they get the hang

of Flying! OFF the porch, on the grass!

They are little birds, Flying—at last!"

"Wow! You do have a great **Front Porch Zoo**!

But one things missing, I think.

Doesn't your zoo have any big cats?"

"Oh, yes, you would have to bring up **that**.

Well, yes. But cats are kind of strange,

And, well, they have a **thing** For wrens.

Do you know what I mean?

So until the wrens are gone,

cats are out of the zoo;

they must Find something else to do."

"So, my little happy Friend,
What do you think of my Front Porch Zoo?"
"Well, I think it's great!
But I have another question For you:
How do I get my mom to start a zoo
just like you?"

"Well, that might take a little time.
But you just be patient and look around.
There are lots of wonderful things just waiting to be Found!"

"By the way, just the other day
I discovered what I thought was a big Fly on a
school's wall.
But to my surprise, it wasn't a Fly at all!
But just to show you nature's variety, what I
thought was a Fly was a cicada at
Angel Oak Elementary!"

"But wait! I have a cicada, too,
right on the porch in my own zoo!
Do they look the same to you?"

"And for another look at variety,
look at this brown mantis on a pine tree,
Again, at Angel Oak Elementary!

But here's a green one for you,
on a red chair in my
Front Porch Zoo."

"Sometimes these little critters will creep inside,
something I know most moms will not abide!
Why, one night I found this toad on my
bathroom window sill!"

"Wow! What did you do to make him shoo?"

"I simply closed the door and went to bed.

And the next morning,
he was on my bathtub instead!
I had nothing to fear, nothing to dread.
He was just a cute little toad.
He wasn't all that bad!"

"That's not what my mom would have said!"

"But now I get it!
Now, I see!
The whole wide world is a zoo,
waiting just For me!"

31

GLOSSARY

Anole, green-a common lizard that can turn different shades of green to brown

Arachnid-a class of animals having eight legs, and a body with two sections, such as spiders and scorpions.

Assassin bug-predator insect, having a large beak with which they pierce other insects to inject poison and eat them

Aviary- a place where birds are kept for viewing or protection and study

Caterpillar-the larva stage of a butterfly or moth

Cicada-a large insect with long, transparent wings, whose male make a loud, high-pitched sound

Disguise(s)-to change one's appearance to hide or conceal one's identity

Hatchlings-birds that are newly hatched out of shell

Herbivores-plant-eating animals

Mantis, praying-large insect that catches its prey with powerful front legs, which gives the appearance of "praying"

Moth-mainly nocturnal insect related to the butterfly, but lacking the clubbed antennae of butterflies.

Scallop-in the shape of the shell of a sea scallop, having curved edges

Serpentarium-a place where generally snakes are kept for viewing in an exhibit

Wren-small, brown song bird having a long pointed beak

RESOURCES

www.softschools.com

www.butterfliesandmoths.org

www.dictionary.com

Acknowledgment:

Special thanks to Suzanne Schumacher, librarian at Angel Oak Elementary School, on Johns Island, South Carolina, for her valuable input and help.

NOTE TO MOMS AND DADS

Except where noted, all photos in this book were taken on or very near my front porch. I am a lover of all things nature. I shot these pictures with my cell phone over a period of a few months. I never considered that they would become a children's book. But I am also a mother, grandmother, and educator. I see the wonder in the eyes of children when they see something that captures their imagination. I also know the challenges that today's parents face. Time is the most precious commodity that a parent has; there seems to be too little of it. The point this book attempts to make is that parents can take a little time and discover big things with their school-aged children, and without the added expense of money! All it takes is a willingness to enjoy the outdoors right in your own backyard or even on your own front porch! You'll be surprised at what you might discover, both on the porch and about your child. Take a little time and enjoy the moment!

Shelia

MEET THE AUTHOR

Shelia L. Anderson, a retired educator, was born in Charleston, South Carolina, where she still resides. She received a Bachelor of Arts degree in English from Winthrop College in Rock Hill, South Carolina, and a Master of Arts degree in English from The Citadel in Charleston, South Carolina. Tapping into "the child within," Anderson explores the natural world right outside her front door to promote reading among elementary school-aged children and enjoying the wonders of nature in their own backyards.

MEET THE ARTIST

J. David Frasier, is a senior at Charleston Southern University. Majoring in Graphic Design. He plans to take his abilities into the field of illustration and advertising. He draws inspiration music, traveling or just interaction with interesting people. This is the second collaboration between him and his mother, the author.

CPSIA information can be obtained
at www.ICGtesting.com
Printed in the USA
BVHW021913200519
548819BV00004B/10/P